15th The King's Hussars

DRESS AND APPOINTMENTS
1759-1914

ALAN KEMP

ALMARK PUBLISHING CO. LTD., LONDON

357. 1

2 023676 21.

By the same author:
AMERICAN SOLDIERS OF THE REVOLUTION

First published—November 1972

ISBN 0 85524 094 6 (hard cover edition)
ISBN 0 85524 095 4 (paper covered edition)

Printed in Great Britain by
Martins Press Ltd., London EC1R 0EN
for the publishers, Almark Publishing Co. Ltd.,
270 Burlington Road, New Malden,
Surrey KT3 4NL, England.

Foreword

THIS book shows the development of the uniforms and equipment of the 15th The King's Hussars from the raising of the Regiment in 1759 to the end of the full-dress era in 1914. Whilst it is not possible in a book of this size to record every order of dress, and the numerous minute alterations over 250 years, all major changes are fully documented.

In the limited space I have tried to give more detailed accounts of the earlier uniforms when items of dress were peculiar only to the 15th. I have not concentrated so much on later orders of dress (eg, khaki frock 1900) as these were common to many regiments at the time and consequently details of them are easier to come by.

The illustrations have been drawn from information collected from contemporary documents and prints, dress regulations and actual items in the possession of the Regiment.

In 1922 the 15th Hussars were amalgamated with the 19th Hussars, forming the 15th/19th The King's Royal Hussars. I regret neglecting the 19th but considered that since so many basic changes of dress affected all hussar regiments, and since the 15th were the elder of the two, a more comprehensive study could be produced by concentrating on them alone.

I should like to extend my thanks to Lieutenant-Colonel J. S. F. Murray, Officer Commanding the 15th/19th The King's Royal Hussars, for allowing me to photograph items of clothing and equipment in the Regiment's possession and for the use of photograph albums. The following is a bibliography of reference sources used in preparing this book:

Military Drawings and Paintings in the Royal Collection (2 Volumes) (Dawnay, Haswell Miller)
History of the Uniforms of the British Army (Lawson)
Journal for the Society of Army Historical Research (various issues)
Dress Regulations and Clothing Orders, 1760 to 1900
Regimental History of the 15th The King's Hussal. (Wylly)
Contemporary paintings, prints and documents
Material in the possession of the Regiment

CONTENTS

*ABOVE: A Lieutenant of the 15th Hussars in Full Dress, 1895.
See text for colour details.*

Introduction

IN 1759 the success of light cavalry troops in Europe prompted Britain to add a light horse regiment to her own army. Raised on March 17, 1759, by Major-General George Augustus Eliott, the Regiment was known as Eliott's Light Dragoons. The raising of the Regiment coincided with a strike of journeymen tailors and many of these men enlisted in the newly formed light horse, causing the Regiment to be known as 'The Tabs'.

The following year Eliott's Light Dragoons were sent to Germany, where the British Army was fighting as the ally of Frederick the Great of Prussia in the Seven Years' War. The Regiment received its baptism of fire on July 16, 1760, at the Battle of Emsdorf, capturing sixteen stands of colours, six cannon and over 2,600 Frenchmen. As a result of the Regiment's remarkable performance it was decided to raise more light dragoon regiments.

George III inspected the Regiment in 1765, bestowing upon it the title of the '15th The King's Light Dragoons'.

In 1793 England was again involved in a war with France which was to drag on for over 20 years. Up to the end of the eighteenth century the 15th Light Dragoons were active on all fronts, distinguishing themselves in Belgium and Holland as well as performing duties in England itself. In March 1807 the Regiment became the '15th The King's Hussars'. It exchanged its light dragoon uniform for the then fashionable Hungarian style costume of the hussars. The 15th added to their battle honours in some classic cavalry actions throughout the Peninsular War, fighting through Portugal, Spain and France right up to the abdication of Napoleon Bonaparte in April 1814.

Sent to Ireland in August of 1814 the 15th was soon recalled when news of Bonaparte's escape from Elba was announced in April 1815. The Regiment sailed for Ostend and formed part of the Fifth Cavalry Brigade under Sir Colquhoun Grant. On June 18, 1815, the 15th Hussars took part in the historic Battle of Waterloo. It was here that Corporal Rolfe of the 15th captured the cloak and pocket-book of Napoleon from the Emperor's carriage.

After the war with France the British Army was greatly reduced in numbers, the 15th Hussars suffering along with the rest. The Regiment was involved in peace-keeping duties during the turbulent years of industrial unrest in the early part of the nineteenth century. The 15th served alternately in England and Ireland until 1839 when they embarked for India. This tour of duty was relatively quiet and lasted until 1854, when the Regiment returned to England. They remained in this country until 1869, leaving again for a second tour in India. Here their time was occupied with little more than inspections and manoeuvres until 1878 when they were mobilized for some very active fighting in the Second Afghan War.

The next conflict involving the 15th Hussars was the Boer War in 1881. After the peace, the Regiment served in the Transvaal on garrison duties, then moved to Natal for a short while before returning to England in 1882.

Seven years later the Regiment found itself in India again, taking part in the

TOP: This picture shows frock coat, stable jacket and full dress. Note the more ornate stable jackets of the Field Officers seated at right of picture. ABOVE: A group of officers of the Regiment, circa 1890, showing frock coats and stable jackets. The two in peaked caps do not belong to the 15th Hussars.

Delhi Durbar of 1903 and acting as escort to visiting personalities.

From India the 15th Hussars moved to South Africa in 1909. Here they were again stationed in the Transvaal on escort and similar duties before being returned to England in January 1913, where they took up duties near Aldershot.

At the outbreak of the Great War in August 1914 three squadrons of the

TOP: The Band of the 15th Hussars in Full Dress, circa 1900. Note the regimental distinction of the crown and lion directly over the rank chevrons of NCOs (Corporals and above). ABOVE: The Band of the 15th Hussars in undress, circa 1900.

15th went to Europe with the first Expeditionary Force. The Regiment served throughout the war on the Western Front, both in a cavalry role and often as infantry in the trenches. In the rearguard action of Villers Cotterets in September 1914, Corporal Garforth of the 15th won a Victoria Cross, one of the first to be awarded in the war.

After the war the Regiment was again sent to Ireland. The country was in the midst of a political upheaval and the 15th were involved in the 'Troubles' until the British withdrawal in 1922. It was in this year that the authorities decided to reduce the number of cavalry regiments in the British Army. The 15th were amalgamated with the 19th Hussars to form the 15th/19th The

King's Royal Hussars.

In 1924 the Regiment went to Egypt, remaining there five years before going on to the North West Frontier of India. Here, under unpleasant conditions, it saw action against hill tribesmen until 1934 when it returned to England.

The development of mechanized weapons in World War I meant that horsed cavalry became obsolete as an effective arm. For some years the transition from horses to armour had been progressing and by August 1939 the 15th/19th Hussars were operational in light tanks and armoured cars.

With the outbreak of war in 1939 the Regiment went to Europe, and were in action until May 1940 when they returned home as part of the army rescued from the beaches at Dunkirk. Returning to France in August 1944 the 15th/19th fought on through Belgium, Holland and Germany. Following the German surrender in May 1945, the Regiment was billeted on the Baltic coast. From here they were moved to Palestine and then Egypt, where they served on security duties before returning to England in 1949. Since 1950 the Regiment or detachments of it have served in many parts of the world, including Germany, Belgium, Transjordan, The Sudan, Malaya, Aden and Northern Ireland.

Drum Horse of the 15th Hussars, circa 1890. The banners have a dark red ground and scrolls with gold lettering, decorations and fringe. The crown is in silver and gold with red cushions and topped with a gold lion. The 'VR' Cypher is embroidered in silver. The shabraque is blue with all lace and embroidery gold, except the crossed flags and hoops of the crown which are silver. The leopard skin has a red teeth edge and the throat plume is scarlet.

The Uniforms

Fig 1: Private, The 15th Light Dragoons, 1760

The dress of the Regiment at this period is well represented in the Morier paintings at Windsor Castle and Wilton House. The helmet consisted of a black enamelled cap with white metal crest and mountings (these are also sometimes shown as copper or brass colour). The crown on the embossed front plate showed red enamel through the hoops. The turban around the base of the cap was dark green and had two white tassels on the ends. The horse-hair mane is usually shown as red, although a letter giving details of the clothing of the Regiment at its raising in 1759 specifies white over red hair.

The red coat had dark green collar, lapels and cuffs, and was lined white. Each lapel had eight white lace loops and white metal buttons set in pairs. The lower part of the sleeves and the coat tails over the pockets each had three chevrons of white tape with buttons in the centre. The collar had a lace and button on each side and there were two buttons on the back of the coat, one above each of the turn-back vents. A white tufted epaulette was sewn on each shoulder. Waistcoat and breeches were white and boots black. The men had brown or black gaiters for dismounted duty. Buff gloves were worn.

Leather equipment consisted of a tan leather pouch on a tan waistbelt, a tan belt (buckled on the back) over the left shoulder on top of the coat with a carbine hanging from a running spring swivel. A second tan belt over the right shoulder (under the coat) carried the sword, which is usually shown as having a simple straight cross-bar hilt or a cross-bar with a slight 'S' shape. Morier shows the sword sometimes as a straight-bladed weapon and sometimes with a slight curve. The scabbard was black leather with metal fittings and the sword knot was white.

The horse furniture consisted of a dark green saddle cloth with a tan leather seat joining the front and rear portions. The edging lace was white with a red centre stripe. The device on the front was a full-colour crown over a white embroidered 'GR'. In each rear corner was a red circle surrounded by natural coloured roses and thistles and with the initials 'LD' in white. The saddle holsters were covered with white fur and the red cloak (which had a green collar) was tied with three straps behind the saddle. It was folded to show the white lining. Reins and straps were black and the stirrups were round with either a two- or three-bar bottom.

Officers' distinctions included a crimson silk sash over the left shoulder (outside the coat) and silver lace and buttons in place of white. Their epaulettes and saddle cloth embroidery were also of silver lace. Paintings of the Regiment by David Morier show some slight variations in uniform details. One, of a charging dragoon, has the collar, lapels and cuffs edged with white. By the Clothing Warrant of 1751 this would indicate that the man is a Sergeant, although his epaulettes appear white rather than the silver of NCOs, and he wears no waist sash. Sashes for Sergeants are listed in Inspection Returns for 1759. Also in this painting, above the wreath on the rear of the shabraque, is a long white scroll bearing the motto 'THE SWIFT, THE VIGILANT AND BOLD' in black. This scroll is not shown on the men's shabraques.

Another of Morier's figures has a white edging tape around the top of the cuffs which was the 1751 instruction for a Corporal's distinction. Many of the paintings omit the button and lace from the collar.

Fig 2: Shabraque and button detail, circa 1760

a

Detail of an officer's shabraque, circa 1763, from a painting by Morier. The cloth is dark green with silver lace edging and a scarlet centre stripe. The trefoil ornaments on front and rear are silver with red inside the loops. The tassels are silver. Holster covers are white fur and the girth is slate covered with brown straps. The saddle is brown leather.

b

This drawing, from a portrait of Lieutenant John Floyd painted about 1763, shows the same shabraque and the officer's distinction of silver lace epaulettes. The uppermost laces on the sleeve and coat tail are set apart from the lower two rather than equidistant as on the men's coats. Facings are dark green and the helmet has a more ornate front plate than that of 1760.

c

Button of the 15th Light Dragoons, circa 1768.

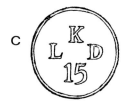

c

b

Fig 3: Private, The 15th The King's Light Dragoons, 1768

Because of their excellent service during the Seven Years' War, the 15th were, in 1766, granted the privilege of wearing the Royal blue for their facings in place of green.

This private of 1768 is similarly dressed to the one of 1760 with the following differences:

The helmet has a more ornate front plate with coloured enamels painted on the embossed metal decoration and the turban is blue.

The coat has an additional white lace and button below the lapels, and now has four laces and buttons set in pairs on the sleeves and coat tails. Buttons were inscribed with the Regiment's initials 'KLD 15'. The epaulettes were now in the facing colour with white edging and tufts. Both cross belts were now worn over the coat and were of white leather, $2\frac{1}{2}$ inches wide. A white

waist belt of $1\frac{3}{4}$-inch width carried a black leather pouch. All buckles and clasps were yellow metal. Black half-gaiters were ordered for officers and men for dismounted duties.

The saddle cloth was now white, having a yellow border with a blue centre stripe. The rear device of the garter, lion and crown were embroidered in red and yellow. The Royal Cypher and the Regiment's identity on the front were embroidered in yellow. The red cloak, lined white, now had a blue collar. Sergeants wore silver braid around the collar and on the buttonholes and epaulettes which had silver fringe. They also wore a waist sash of crimson spun silk with a centre stripe of the facing colour. Corporals wore similar epaulettes to the Sergeants and had narrow silver lace around the turn-up of the cuffs.

Officers wore two silver embroidered fringed epaulettes and a crimson silk waist sash tied on the right and worn under the coat. Lace was silver although some officers did not have their buttonholes laced at all. Saddle embroidery was also silver in place of white, and gilt in place of yellow. Sword belts were to be of white leather for officers, worn over the right shoulder under the coat, but a portrait of Cornet James Lumsdaine of the Regiment, painted prior to 1770, shows a metallic belt with a centre stripe of blue. As late as May 1772 sword belts were still reported as being blue velvet with silver embroidery.

After 1766 Light Dragoons had replaced side drums with brass trumpets (bugle horns for field calls) decorated with crimson mixed blue trumpet cords. The trumpeters of the 15th wore red coats faced blue with yellow and blue lace. They wore hats with red feathers rather than helmets, were mounted on greys and carried scimitar bladed swords.

Fig 4: Two helmets of the 15th Light Dragoons

It is not clear which of the helmets was worn first. That on the left has an inscription around the edge of the peak which reads: 'Five Battalions of French Defeated and taken by this Regiment with their Colours and Nine Pieces of Cannon, on the Plains of Emsdorf, July the Sixteenth 1760'. It also bears the motto 'Merebimur', which was not granted until 1766. All the embellishments are embossed and are copper on a black ground.

The second helmet has neither the inscription or the Merebimur motto and the guidons are enamelled red and yellow with the Bourbon flags (outer) in white. The garter scroll and lion are enamelled yellow and the crown is yellow with a red cushion. The construction of this helmet is better than that of the other.

12

An officer in a portrait of 1790 wears this second type (see Fig 5) which could indicate that this pattern was for officers and the other for men.
In both examples the turbans are blue and the horsehair crests red.

Fig 5: Head-dress and badge detail

a   *An officer of the 15th, from a painting of about 1790. The two jackets are blue laced silver with red shoulder wings. The obsolete metal helmet is worn (see Fig 4).*

b   *This drawing is from a contemporary engraving of James Leishman, a Quartermaster of the Regiment from 1760–1799. It gives a good indication of the lace pattern on the underjacket.*

c *Helmet plate from the 1784 cap. Worn on the right side above the turban, the badge was silver for officers and white metal for the men.*

d *Officer's silver cross-belt plate, circa 1795.*

Fig 6: Sergeant, The 15th The King's Light Dragoons, 1799

A General Order of July 1796 altered the cut of the light cavalry jacket. The new design was waist length without skirts and with parallel lines of braid across the front looped at the outsides and having three rows of buttons. For the 15th the jacket was blue with red collar and cuffs trimmed white (all braid was silver for Sergeants and officers). The seams on the back of the jacket were also decorated with braid and loops. The shoulder wings of 1790 had now disappeared. The helmet is the same as that shown on the private of 1793 (see colour plate 2) but now has an all-scarlet plume, a distinction granted to the Regiment in April 1799. Hair powder was no longer used by NCOs and men after July 1795 except for Sundays and reviews. The Sergeant's crimson waist sash had a centre stripe of the facing colour. He also wore two chevrons in the facing colour on the right upper arm (the Stubb's painting of a Sergeant of the 10th Light Dragoons agrees with this but in the picture the chevrons have an edging of silver). An alternative source specifies 'a double row of vellum lace of the colour of the horse furniture of the Regiment' for chevrons. Corporals had a single chevron.

Breeches were white and the top of the boot was trimmed with braid and tassel. The shoulder belt was white leather and carried a black leather pouch and a running swivel for the carbine. The stirrup hilted sword in a steel scabbard was worn slung from a white waist belt with a 'snake' clasp. Holsters and saddle cloth were as before, but the blue cloak now had sleeves. When dismounted the men wore blue overalls strapped with leather and a black leather forage cap of mitre shape. Long black gaiters were worn on foot parades.

Since 1796 officers had been ordered to wear 'scale epaulettes and wings', but there is little evidence to show whether the 15th adopted these, although Dighton in his caricature paintings shows an officer of the Regiment with some sort of metallic shoulder decoration.

Fig 7: Sketches of officers from contemporary paintings

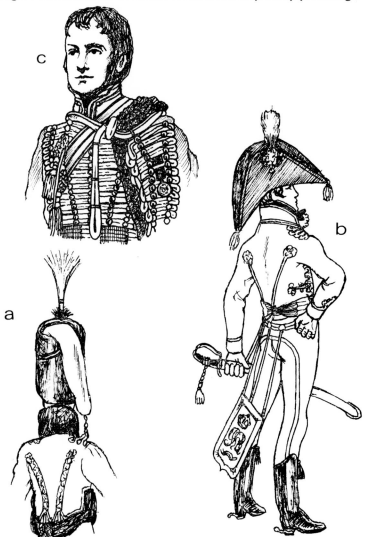

a   *After Dighton, circa 1808. Black busby, white over red plume, red bag. Blue jacket laced silver, black fur.*

b   *After Dighton, circa 1803. Black hat, silver lace on cockade, gold tassels white over red plume. Blue jacket laced silver, red collar and cuffs. Blue breeches laced silver. Black boots. Gold and red barrel sash. Belt and slings red, laced gold. Sabretache red, edged in gold lace with decorations silver. Sword in steel scabbard with red and gold knot.*

c   *From an oil painting, circa 1818. Blue jackets, laced silver, red collar, black fur. Gold belt with scarlet stripes. This officer wears his Waterloo medal looped through the lace on the pelisse.*

**Fig 8: Private,
The 15th The King's
(Light Dragoons)
Hussars, 1806**

Although the change-over from Light Dragoons to Hussars is usually given as 1805, an extract from the 'Adjutant's Journal' dated June 1804 lists the receipt of 50 hussar caps and 520 white cap lines.

The new uniform of the 15th was a waist-length blue jacket (dolman) with scarlet collar and cuffs trimmed with white braid. The front of the jacket was also braided white (with white metal buttons), as were the seams on the back. An over-jacket (pelisse) was also worn, usually slung over the left shoulder. This was also blue and was trimmed around the edge and on the cuffs with black fur. It had two rows of white metal buttons on the right side and one on the left. The garment was braided across in the manner of the dolman and, when worn as a jacket, was fastened with braid loops which linked over from the left side to the buttons on the right. A white cord below the collar fastened around the neck when the pelisse was worn slung. In November 1806 Sergeants requested that they may be permitted to furnish their own pelisses and reports that the Sergeants' fur was lighter than the regimental black could indicate that permission was granted. The white leather shoulder belt carried a black leather pouch and a running swivel for the carbine, which now had only a 21-inch barrel. The curved sword with stirrup hilt hung on slings from a white leather waist belt with 'snake' clasp, which also held the black leather sabretache. The barrel sash was of crimson and yellow spun worsted, tied behind with a toggle and cords which were looped up on the right side of the waist. Breeches were white with black boots. It was, however, found necessary to wear overalls to preserve the breeches. An Order of December 1806 instructs the men to wear blue overalls out of barracks and white trousers in. The blue overalls had a stripe of the facing colour on the outside seams with buttons over the stripe and chains looped under the soles of the boots.

The head-dress of the Hussars was now a tall fur cap with yellow cords, but often alternative caps were worn to preserve the fur. The 15th appear to have worn a black undress shako some 8 inches deep with a top diameter of 11 inches. The shako was decorated with white braid, loop and wheel and was sometimes worn with a white plume. Some officers wore scarlet shakos with silver trim, a forerunner of things to come. (continued on page 18)

16

Plate 1: Drummer and French hornist, 1760
The red and green rosettes on the horse and helmets are often omitted from similar contemporary paintings of the Regiment and are believed to be additional badges worn by recruiting parties. The hanging sleeves behind the Drummer's shoulders are scarlet, edged white, and had chevrons of lace like the coat sleeves backed scarlet.

Horse furniture consisted of a blue cloth shabraque with a scarlet vandyked border. At front and rear was the King's Cypher and Crown embroidered in yellow and red above inverted white flags bearing yellow fleur-de-lis. Between the cypher and crown was a scarlet scroll with the legend 'Merebimur' in yellow. The white sheep-skin was edged with scarlet cloth teeth and the valise behind the saddle was of blue cloth with edging trim and initials in red.

In 1801 NCOs of the 15th Hussars had been granted Royal permission to wear a crown above the rank chevrons. Two years later the rank markings for NCOs were changed to four chevrons for a Sergeant-Major, three for a Sergeant and two for a Corporal. The lace for Sergeants and Corporals of the Regiment was to be 'yellow with a central blue stripe' (ie, Royal Lace).

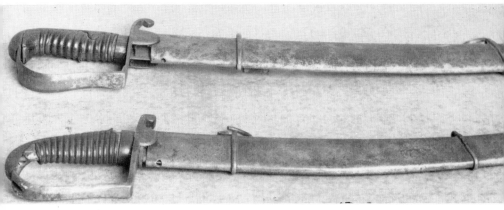

Fig 9: Officer's and trooper's swords, 1808

Two swords of the 15th carried at Sahagun in 1808. In the foreground is an officer's model. The hilt is steel with the wooden grip covered in black leather. The 28-inch blade has a sharp curve.

The second sword is that of a trooper. It is not so curved as the officer's and has a 34-inch blade. The hilt is steel with wooden grip covered with leather.

Fig 10: Officer, The 15th The King's Light Dragoons (Hussars), 1808

The officer shown here is in Review Order. The dolman and pelisse are styled much the same as those in Fig 8, but with the rows of braiding in silver lace closer together and more decorative than the men's. The weight of lace increased in quantity with the rank and both jackets had for officers five rows of buttons rather than three. The pelisse was lined with crimson silk and had heavy silver cords to suspend it around the shoulders. A scarlet waistcoat, laced silver, was also worn by officers. The pouch belt was scarlet leather with stripes of silver lace, as was the sword belt and slings (gold lace is often shown in contemporary paintings in place of silver). The pouch was of scarlet cloth richly embroidered in gold. The sabretache of red leather was faced with scarlet cloth with silver lace border and silver and gold embroidery. The sash was of crimson silk cord with gold 'barrels' and tassels. Breeches were white buckskin, worn with black knee boots edged and tasselled silver. Gloves were white.

The busby was of dark fur with a scarlet bag and a white plume tufted red at the base. Cap lines were gold, plaited together around the top of the cap and hanging in three large flounders with tassels. It was worn at first without chin scales, but these were added later.

The black sheepskin had a scarlet scalloped edge and the shabraque was dark blue, edged scarlet, with scalloped edged silver lace and tassels at the rear ends. The double Royal Cyphers were silver with gold crowns worked scarlet. The scarlet scroll on top carried the word 'Merebimur' in silver embroidery and the lower scroll was inscribed 'Emsdorf'. Below this decoration on the rear corners were two inverted flags in silver bearing gold fleur-de-lis.

The saddles and black head harness of the officers' mounts were decorated with silver and scarlet leather and had black rosettes decorated silver with scarlet centres.

In undress the officers wore blue-grey overalls with a double scarlet stripe on the outside seams.

Fig 11: Officer, The 15th The King's Light Dragoons (Hussars), 1819

Although the busby of the 15th Hussars was replaced by a scarlet shako in 1812, the Regiment was in the Spanish Peninsula at the time and did not receive them until early in 1813. It is not certain why scarlet was chosen for the 15th when other regiments received black. One theory is that it was a reminder of the scarlet plume granted in 1799. Another is that it was in memory of Hompesch's Mounted Riflemen, a disbanded Emigré regiment which had worn scarlet caps and whose Colonel, R. B. Long, was a Lieutenant-Colonel of the 15th Hussars. The officer's shako was decorated with gold lace and the men's with yellow, although the top band is often shown as silver and white respectively. The falling red and white horsehair plume was worn by both.

The jacket was still blue with red collar and cuffs, laced silver, although by 1819 'chain lace' is recorded as having replaced cord on the uniform. The pelisse remained blue, laced silver, with black fur.

The pantaloons for full dress were of blue cloth having one broad lace, edged by two narrow silver laces on the outside seams, joining in a decorative knot across the seat. On each thigh was a heavily embroidered Austrian knot in silver regimental lace. In undress, grey overalls with ankle boots were worn. The overalls had a silver lace stripe on the outside seams (white for the men). The pouch, sword belt and sabretache slings were now red, laced gold in place of silver, although the pouch itself was silver laced. The sabretache of red leather was also now trimmed in gold lace on a scarlet cloth ground.

The shabraque was much the same as that shown on the figures of 1815 (colour plate), but with a scalloped red edge on the inside of the silver lace edging as well as on the outside.

Plate 2: Officer, 1784 and Private, 1793
(description on page 22)

Plate 3: Officer, 1808
(description on page 23)

Plate 2: Officer 1784 and Private 1793, The 15th The King's Light Dragoons

The Clothing Warrant of 1784 resulted in a complete change of uniform for Light Dragoons.

A new short-tailed blue jacket with white lining had red cuffs and stand-up collar. Epaulettes appear to have varied considerably, ranging from laced shoulder straps to panels of metal, lace or chain. For officers the jacket was trimmed with a profusion of silver braid and tassels. It was worn over another short blue jacket, also trimmed with silver braid. The over-jacket had two long cords below the collar which could be tied enabling it to be worn as a slung cape. A crimson waist sash was knotted on the right. Breeches were of white buckskin and boots were black. White gloves were worn.

The sword belt was white with a silver belt plate. It was worn over the right shoulder with a stirrup hilted sword hanging from two white slings. An Inspection Return of October 1775 states that swords had been re-hilted in 1773, presumably replacing the simple cross-bar hilt. The sword knot was silver worked with red (the new facing colour).

A new pattern head-dress, known as the 'Light Dragoon helmet', was introduced. It was made of japanned leather with a leather peak, edged in silver metal. The turban, in the facing colour red, was held by fine silver chains and had a narrow silver plate across the front inscribed '15th Light Dragoons'. On the right side of the helmet, above the turban, was a silver regimental badge. The cap was topped by a bearskin crest and had a white over red vertical plume on the left side. As late as 1788 a report stated that the 15th Light Dragoons were still wearing their old metal helmets with horsehair manes in that year. Evidence supporting this may be found in a contemporary painting of an officer standing with a civilian group. His top and under-jackets are undoubtedly those of the 1784 pattern, but his scarlet shoulder wings would date the picture as post-1790 when wings were ordered. The lace pattern differs slightly in shape from that described in regimental notes, but the officer is doubtless of the 15th as his helmet clearly indicates.

Officers are reputed to have worn a scarlet cloth pouch and shoulder belt embroidered silver (not shown in this plate) and a black patent leather sabretache was introduced for the first time.

The uniform of the men was similar to that of the officers, but with white lace and metal in place of silver. Sergeants wore silver lace. The saddle holsters were topped with black fur and the rolled blue cape had a red collar and lining. The shabraque, when worn, would be the 1768 pattern.

The uniform of the private of this period is similar to that of the officer of 1784. The Clothing Warrant of that year specified that unlike the officers' jackets those of the men were to be 'shells' without sleeves, to be worn over the sleeved waist jacket. Beneath this was yet another garment, a sleeved under-waistcoat of coarse grey flannel piped down the front, collar and cuffs with blue braid and buttoned inside the waistband of the breeches.

The shell jacket for the men was without tassels on the white braiding. By 1793 the scarlet collar, cuffs and shoulder flaps were edged white and wings in the facing colour (red) with white edging had been added. The badges on the helmet were in white metal and the turban was in the facing colour. Pouch and belts were white leather with steel scabbard and stirrup hilted sword. Holster covers were black fur and the rolled cloak was now blue, having been changed from red in 1786. Black half-gaiters were worn for dismounted duty. It was in 1794 that the distinctive regimental lace, 'the Austrian Wave' was adopted.

Plate 3: Officer, 1808

This is a copy of a water-colour in the Regiment's possession. A similar painting of an officer on foot (signed Dighton), and also belonging to the Regiment, shows what is presumably undress uniform. The lace is gold rather than silver and the overalls are light blue with brown leather booting, and white stripes on the outside seams. The sabretache is black without ornaments and all belts are white, as is the sword knot.

Plate 4: Officer and Private, 1815

A number of hussar regiments wore the busby at Waterloo, but the 15th appear to have worn their scarlet shakos without the oilskin covers.

Plate 5: Officer, Review Order, 1822 and Private in Marching Order, 1828

In April 1822 a new uniform was specified for the 15th Hussars. The entire jacket, including collar and cuffs, was now blue. The Prussian collar was 3 inches deep, as were the pointed cuffs. Both were richly ornamented with silver regimental lace and Russian tracing braid. The same lace was laid all around the edges of the jacket and on the welts and seams. Across the chest were 16 or 17 rows of matt silver lace interspersed with lines of bright silver braid to the second button on each side. The lace spanned the whole of the chest below the collar, narrowing to about 3-inch width at the bottom of the jacket. Of the five rows of silver buttons the centre row were 'balls' and the other four rows 'half-balls'. The jacket had a white silk lining.

The pelisse was also blue similarly laced with a 4-inch collar of black fur and 3-inch deep fur cuffs. The bottom was also edged in fur which was let into the lace on the sleeves and welts. Matt silver necklines with bright silver slides and olivets hung from the collar. The pelisse was lined with crimson silk. Field Officers had wide lace and more complex figuring on the sleeves. A white kerseymere waistcoat was worn with ball buttons and silver lace trimming on the collar, welts and edges.

The leg-wear was as follows—Full Dress: Scarlet pantaloons with a stripe of silver regimental lace between two stripes of tracing braid on each outside seam. This lace went across the seat in a decorative figure. Austrian knots of silver lace and braid were worked on each thigh. Black hessian boots with silver lace and tassels were worn. Dress: Scarlet Cossack overalls with stripes of regimental lace up the outside seams to the waistband worn with black ankle boots. Undress: Grey Cossack overalls with a single scarlet cloth stripe up each outside seam to the waistband, worn with black ankle boots. Silver-plated spurs were worn in all three orders of dress. The $8\frac{1}{2}$-inch high scarlet shako had a diameter across the top of $10\frac{1}{2}$ inches. Around the top was a $2\frac{1}{2}$-inch band of gold lace. (This was peculiar only to the 15th, other regiments having inter-secting circles of gold braid.) Gold braid was edged around the bottom of the cap, around the edge of the black patent leather peak and the edge of a turned-up black peak at the back. The front of the shako carried a gold braid wheel with a chain loop and buttons. At the top was a gold cord rosette with a scarlet centre. The cap lines and flounders were gold and the chin scales silver (these were held by lion-head motifs well up on the sides of the cap). In full dress and dress the shako had a black drooping plume of cocktail feathers (black horsehair for undress).

(Continued on page 26)

Plate 4: Officer and Private, 1815
(description on page 23)

24

Plate 5: Officer, Review Order, 1822 and Private in Marching Order, 1828
(description on page 23)

In 1821 a tall plume of red and white vulture feathers had been adopted (horsehair for the men) but this was soon discarded in favour of the cock-feathers. A Dighton painting of the Duke of York's review on June 1, 1822, shows the men of the 15th wearing white over red upright plumes. The barrel sash was crimson and gold. The 2-inch wide pouch belt of gold lace had a crimson stripe down the centre with a thin crimson stripe on each edge. It was lined scarlet with a gilt buckle, tip and slide and had silver ornaments and chains on the chest. The pouch of scarlet cloth had a gold embroidered double 'GR' surmounted by a crown in the centre, embroidered around with gold braid. The sword belt and slings were scarlet Morocco leather with gold lace trim, and the clasp fastening and mountings were gilt. The dress sabretache was 15 inches deep of red leather with a scarlet cloth face embroidered with gold lace. The regulation sabre was worn on all parade and mounted duties. The Mameluke hilted sword on full-dress occasions.

The jacket and pelisse were both blue, lined white and laced across with 18 double loops of white braid. The fill-in braid between the chest lace, which gave a solid front effect on the officer's uniform, was absent from the jacket and pelisse of the men. In place of fur the pelisse was edged around the fronts and bottom with black wool. It also had a black wool collar, cuffs and hip insets. It had an edge tracing of white cord above the wool and on the back seams. On the left side of the pelisse was one row of buttons and on the right two. When worn over the jacket it was linked with four hooks and eyes. Double cords at the collar were worn around the neck when the pelisse was slung on the shoulder. In 1830 the cord was changed from white to yellow. Contrary to an Order of 1823 for cavalry to wear blue-grey overalls, the 15th were permitted to continue wearing dark grey. In 1822 NCOs and men had been ordered to wear stripes of the regimental facing colour on the outside seam of the overalls, but most contemporary evidence shows a white stripe.

Although major changes in the dress of the 15th did not occur until 1831, Regimental Orders of 1827 specified 'scarlet Cossack overalls with gold lace appointments' and Hull's plate of an officer of 1828 also shows gold. The scarlet shako (which was reduced in height in 1828) was trimmed in yellow braid and cords and had a black horsehair plume. The barrel sash was crimson and yellow with crimson cords, and the shoulder and sword belts were of white leather. The pouch was black leather.

The standing figure in the colour plate for 1828 shows the Marching Order of dress for men, with the shako covered by a black oilskin. The shabraque would be blue with yellow braid and embroidery, and would be doubled up upon the croup in marching order.

The sword was that adopted in 1822 and was less curved than that previously used. It had a 35-inch blade with a half-basket hilt, a steel scabbard and white knot. The carbine had been changed in 1825 to one with a barrel length of only 15 inches. A fixed suspension ring replaced the sliding one.

Plate 6: Officer and Trumpeter, Full Dress, 1834

In August 1831, William IV, 'the Sailor King', decided that the colour blue should be reserved for naval uniforms and that red was more fitting for the army. This ruling was, however, only partially adhered to by most of those regiments affected. Hussars exchanged their blue pelisses for scarlet ones, but retained their blue jackets.

In an effort to reduce the enormous cost involved in clothing hussar officers, the August Order stated that 'the four regiments of Hussars are to be perfectly alike. The officers to have one dress only, and that of a less costly pattern which will forthwith be prepared'. The new dress involved less lace embroidery than before and only three rows of buttons in place of the usual five on both jacket and pelisse. Officers of the hussar regiments, however, protested at the proposed austerity and the Order was rescinded before the end of 1831. If the marked lack of pictorial evidence of the proposed new uniform is a true indication, it would appear that none of the hussar regiments ever wore the 'three-button' jacket or pelisse. The uniform of 1831 was then, very similar to the previous one except for the scarlet pelisse and all lace and buttons now being gold instead of silver.

The scarlet shako was again reduced slightly in height and had a sunken top of 11 inches diameter. Around the top was a 2-inch wide gold lace with three narrow crimson lines. The bottom of the cap was bound with a thinner gold lace and the black patent leather peak had a gold edging. The leather turn-up peak on the rear of the shako had disappeared. The front centre had a wheel and loop in gold lace which went to the top of the shako, meeting the large gold rosette with a crimson centre. Above this was a gilt 'tulip' which held a plume of black cock-tail feathers.

The overalls were now dark blue with single stripe of gold lace $1\frac{1}{2}$ inches wide down each outside seam. These were worn with ankle boots and gilt spurs. Gloves were white leather. The barrel sash was as before and the sword belt and slings were 1-inch wide gold lace, edged red on a backing of leather. The belt had a decorative clasp fastening. The sabretache of red leather had a scarlet cloth face embroidered with gold lace.

The pouch belt was also gold lace with scarlet edging and ornamented buckle, tip and slide. The pouch was of scarlet cloth richly embroidered with gold and silver lace and with gold lace edging.

The Mameluke dress sword had been officially discontinued in May 1831 but was worn sporadically until a further Order of December 1892 finally removed it.

The shabraque was entirely different to that of the 1820s being now of scarlet cloth, diagonally shaped in front and embroidered with the crown over the double 'WR' cypher. The rear end had a point 3 feet 9 inches deep embroidered with a larger crown and cypher. Between these was a triple blue silk scroll with gold edge bearing the honours 'Egmont-Op-Zee', 'Emsdorf', and 'Villiers-en-Couch' in gold. On the left of the cypher was a similar scroll with 'Sahagun' and on the right one with 'Vittoria'. Below the 'WR' was the Regiment's badge of a lion and crown flanked by two more blue silk scrolls, the left inscribed 'Peninsula' and the right 'Waterloo'. Below this were the inverted Bourbon flags in silver with gold fleur-de-lys. Below the flags the number '15' and below this 'KH' in gold. The shabraque had a thin red edge around the outside and a $2\frac{1}{2}$-inch border of gold lace. Over the shabraque in full dress was worn a black sheep-skin with a scalloped red edge. The horse furniture was decorated with gold and red rosettes and a scarlet throat plume was worn.

(Continued on page 30)

Plate 6: Officer and Trumpeter, Full Dress, 1834
(description on page 27)

**Plate 7: Private in Full Dress, 1868 and Private
in Stable Dress, 1890**
(description on page 30)

A leopard-skin was reputedly the saddle cover for undress, but prints of the period show officers in full dress with a leopard-skin over the dress shabraque rather than the black sheep-skin. To further complicate matters one illustration of an officer of 1831 in Field Day order (with covered shako and buttoned pelisse) shows a black sheep-skin over a plain blue shabraque which has a large red vandyked edge.

The Trumpeter shown in this plate wears a scarlet horsehair plume rather than the black of the men.

Apart from the restoration of the blue pelisse in place of scarlet in 1841, the full dress of the Regiment altered little until 1855. In this year a completely new type of jacket was ordered. It consisted of a blue single-breasted tunic with a 2-inch deep collar rounded in front and braided and laced in gold. Down the chest were six loops of gold chain lace ending in gold caps and drops. The loops narrowed toward the waist from 8 inches at the top to 4 inches at the bottom. The jacket was fastened with six olivets worked in gold. The entire jacket was edged around in gold chain lace. Each seam on the back had a double chain of gold lace triple looped at the top and knotted at the bottom with a gold cap over each lace at the waist. The skirt, which was lined black, was $9\frac{1}{2}$ inches long. The pelisse and barrel sash were abolished and the sword belt was now worn under the jacket. The shako now had a height and diameter of just over 7 inches.

Plate 7: Private in Full Dress, 1868 and Private in Stable Dress, 1890

The early forage caps were of blue cloth and somewhat larger than the later pillboxes. The colour was changed to scarlet in 1834. Drawings of about 1855 show privates with blue bands around the caps, while the Regimental Sergeant-Major and the Trumpeters have yellow. Shortly after this date all other ranks wore yellow, the officers wearing gold lace.

Fig 12: Officer (undress), 1822

There were a number of differences between the full and the undress uniforms of this period. The blue undress jacket had a 3-inch deep collar ornamented with broad and narrow silver lace. Down the front were five decorated silver cord loops with roses on each side and a centre row of olivets. There was an edging of silver cord around the jacket and broad and narrow silver cord trimmed the cuffs, hips and welts. The blue cloth pelisse had a 4-inch deep fur collar and 3-inch fur cuffs. It was edged in fur with inlets of fur on the sleeves and welts. The decoration of silver lace was similar to that on the jacket and it carried neck lines and slides in silver.

Grey overalls of Cossack cut (cut very full, diminishing in width towards the foot) with a single scarlet stripe on the outside seam were worn. The black ankle boots had silver-plated spurs. The pouch belt for undress was $2\frac{1}{2}$ inches wide of black patent leather with a pouch of the same material, $4\frac{1}{2}$ inches deep $\times$ $6\frac{1}{4}$ inches wide, and having rounded corners. Like the dress belt it was decorated with chest ornaments in silver. The undress sword belt and slings were of 1-inch wide Russian leather embroidered silver. From these hung a new pattern sword, much less curved than its predecessor. It had a 35-inch blade, a half-basket steel hilt with two fluted bars on the outside and the black fishskin grip was bound with wire. The scabbard was steel and the knot white. The sabretache for undress was black patent leather, 12 inches deep $\times$ 8 inches wide at the top sloping to $10\frac{1}{2}$ inches wide at the bottom. It had no ornaments. At this time the forage cap was blue cloth with a top decoration and band of silver braid.

Fig 13: Officer's pelisse, circa 1829

Field Officers had wider lace and more ornate figuring braid. An interesting feature is that the trim is Astrakhan rather than fur, although the braiding appears too decorative for an undress pelisse.

Plate 8: Lieutenant in Review Order, 1905 and Sergeant in Khaki Frock, India 1901

(description on page 33)

Plate 8: Lieutenant in Review Order, 1905 and Sergeant in Khaki Frock, India, 1901

The Colonial pattern helmet did not carry the cap lines. These were looped up on the right of the chest, fastened around the neck and led under the left arm to the second top row of lace on the front. All lace was gold except the stripes on the breeches, which were of yellow cloth. The Sergeant wears the field service cap. Those of the men did not have the edging braid on the flap.

Fig 14: Officer's Horse Equipment, circa 1829

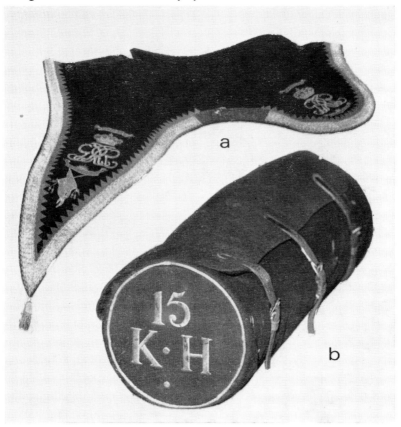

a *The shabraque (colour details on page 23).*
b *Saddle valise. Blue trimmed silver.*

Fig 15: Lacing detail, circa 1825

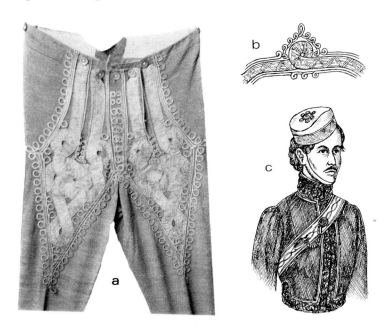

a
b
c

a *Officer's full dress pantaloons of fine scarlet web. The thigh ornaments are of silver lace. Circa 1825.*
b *Design of lace on seat of pantaloons. The lace, edged with tracing braid, runs down each outside seam.*
c *Drawing of an officer in undress from a water-colour in possession of the Regiment and dated 1838. The cap is scarlet with gold lace and ornament. The dark blue jacket is trimmed with black braid and Astrakhan. The shoulder belt is gold worked with scarlet and has gold ornaments and chains.*

Fig 16: Officer's barrel sash of crimson silk cord and gold

This example dates from about 1825, but there was little variation in pattern during the whole period in which barrel sashes were worn.

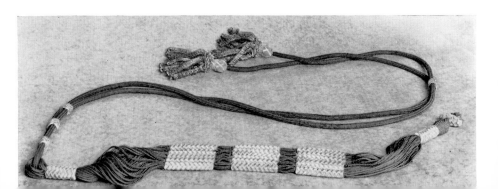

Fig 17: Officer's Dress Sabretaches

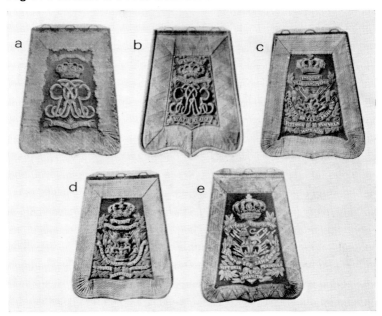

a   *1806–1817   Red leather, faced with scarlet cloth, with a silver lace border and silver and gold embroidery.*
b   *1817–1830.*
c   *Circa 1830–1837.*
d   *1837–1841.*
e   *1841–1902.*
    The last four have gold lace and embroidery on scarlet cloth.

Fig 18: Horse furniture and stable dress, circa 1840

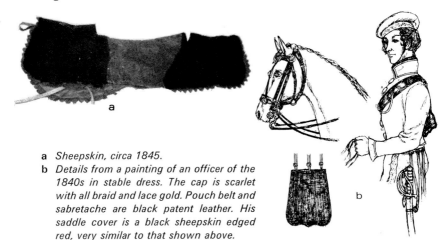

a   *Sheepskin, circa 1845.*
b   *Details from a painting of an officer of the 1840s in stable dress. The cap is scarlet with all braid and lace gold. Pouch belt and sabretache are black patent leather. His saddle cover is a black sheepskin edged red, very similar to that shown above.*

35

Fig 19: Details of Marching Order Dress
(from a painting by J. Fearnley of about 1851)

a

a   *The officers in the painting have the cap lines wound around the shako but no edging around the peak. The NCOs and men wear the cap lines hanging loose and do have a peak edging. All ranks wear the oilskin cover.*

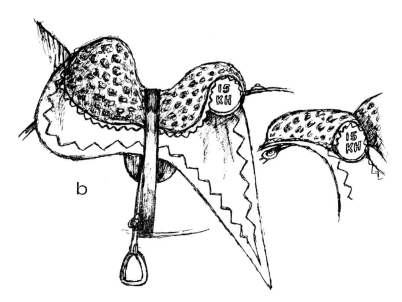

b

b   *An undress shabraque for officers was introduced in 1846. It consisted of a plain blue cloth with a scarlet vandyked border. It was covered by a red-edged leopard-skin cut square at the rear to cover the blue valise (trimmed red). Men's shabraques are embroidered. The officers wear embroidered pouch belts and richly laced jackets, but have plain black patent leather sabretaches. All ranks wear the slung pelisse and white gloves.*

Fig 20: Officer, The 15th The King's Hussars, 1868

Two years after the introduction of the new jacket some alterations were ordered. Cuffs were to be 10½ inches round and the sleeve ornaments were reduced from 8 inches to 7 inches for Subalterns, from 8¾ inches to 8 inches for Captains, and from 11 inches to 8 inches for Field Officers.

The scarlet shako was finally laid to rest and replaced by a black sable fur busby which sloped from 7¾ inches in front to 9 inches at the rear. On the front of the cap, level with the top, was a 2-inch deep gold gimp oval cockade. Above this a plume of scarlet osprey feathers (with a gilt ring) rose to a height of 8 inches from upright gold leaves on a gilt corded ball. A scarlet cloth bag, hanging on the right side of the busby, was trimmed around the seam and down the centre line with gold braid. At the bottom, where the braids met, was a 1-inch gold gimp button. Under the bag, at the top of the cap, was a gilt ring to hold the cap lines and a gilt hook to loop up the gilt chin chain. The cap lines of gold pearl cord with slides led from under the bag to around the neck with the olive ends fastened on the right of the chest. Reputedly the 15th Hussars have not since 1812 worn the cap lines wound around the busby as in other hussar regiments, but prints and photographs show otherwise.

In 1859 the shabraque was changed from scarlet to blue cloth, cut square in front and pointed behind. The length was 4 feet 4 inches and the officers' model was edged in gold lace with the cypher 'VR' with the crown over on the front corners and the crown over the Queen's crest within the garter surrounded by the word 'Merebimur'. Under this were the inverted crossed Bourbon flags and beneath '15H'. All embroidery was gold except the flags, which were silver.

In April of the following year the yellow stripe on the officer's overalls was changed to one of gold lace. Changes were made to the horse furniture in 1864. A scarlet horsehair throat decoration, 18 inches long, hung from the bridle in a brass ball and socket. Over the saddle was worn a 3 foot 4 inch long black lambskin, edged with scarlet cloth teeth. The blue cloth valise was 27 inches long and $6\frac{1}{2}$ inches in diameter with the edging, initials and number of the Regiment embroidered in gold. In 1871 the booted overalls were replaced by breeches and boots. 1873 saw the abolition of shabraques for NCOs and men (their sheepskins remained in use until 1897).

In 1874 the tunic decoration was altered from 'gold chain lace' to 'gold chain gimp', an Austrian knot being added to the bottom of each back seam lace touching the bottom of the skirt and the gimp traced all around with gold braid. Each cuff had an Austrian knot 8 inches in length. The skirts were rounded in front. Field Officers had figured braiding below the collar lace and around the sleeve knot (11 inches long). Captains had braided eyes below the lace on the collar and around the sleeve knot (8 inches long). Two $\frac{3}{4}$-inch wide stripes of gold lace ($\frac{1}{4}$-inch apart) ran down the seams of the blue cloth overalls and pantaloons.

The scarlet plume on the busby was 9 inches high from the top of the cap. Slings for sword and sabretaches were now only $\frac{1}{2}$-inch wide and the lace around the sabretache was reduced to $2\frac{1}{2}$ inches wide.

In full dress, brass spurs were worn and in undress spurs of steel. The shabraque was like that of 1859, but now had two $\frac{3}{4}$-inch wide stripes of gold lace ($\frac{1}{4}$-inch apart) around the edge. The leopard-skin saddle cover was retained.

In 1883, plaited gold shoulder straps with a small button near the collar were added to the tunic. The rank badges were moved from the collar and now worn on these straps. The rank markings were as follows:

Colonel	— Crown with two pips below
Lieutenant-Colonel	— Crown with one pip
Major	— Crown
Captain	— Two pips
Lieutenant	— One pip
Second-Lieutenant	— Plain shoulder strap

For mounted duties knee boots with V-cut tops and gold bosses were worn with steel spurs. In full and levee dress blue cloth pantaloons with $\frac{3}{4}$-inch gold lace traced each side with gold braid were worn with similar boots, which had the addition of $\frac{3}{4}$-inch gold lace around the edge. Gilt spurs were worn with these.

The gold lace on the sword belt and slings had an $\frac{1}{8}$-inch scarlet stripe added to the centre. Unlike other hussar regiments at this time the 15th did not adopt chains and prickers on the front of the pouch belt.

In levee dress special busby lines were worn. These were plaited for 10 inches across the front of the cap and had gold acorns on the ends. A scarlet cloth field service cap was worn in service dress.

In 1893, the busby was reduced in height ($6\frac{1}{4}$ inches in front, $7\frac{3}{4}$ inches at rear) with the egret plume 13 inches high above the top of the cap. The sabretache was to be no longer than 12 inches.

The steel collar chains on officers' chargers were changed for head ropes in 1893. The following year the overall stripes for officers were altered from gold lace to yellow cloth, although on the levee dress pantaloons a single cord of gold gimp was worn. Slings and belts for undress were of white (buff) leather.

In 1896, blue serge frocks for undress with brass buttons and steel shoulder chains were worn. Brown gloves were introduced. Seven years later the shoulder chains were abolished.

1904 saw considerable changes made to the equipment. The sabretache and shabraque were both abolished (the NCOs and men had been without sabretaches since 1888). Officers' saddles were now covered by a leopard skin with an embroidered scarlet patch on the front. A drab mixture cloth greatcoat of universal pattern was adopted. The foreign service uniform was a khaki jacket (frock), breeches and puttees (officers wore brown leather gaiters). The Sam Browne belt, which had previously been worn only on service in India, was now generally adopted for officers.

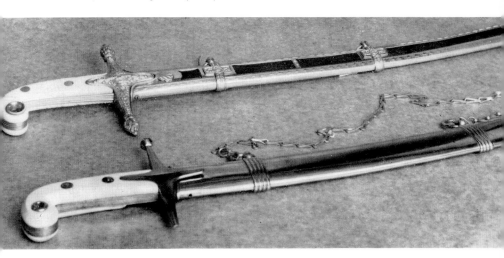

Fig 21 : Officers' Mameluke sabres

The sword in the foreground has a 33-inch blade. The hilt is polished steel with ivory grips (one end of the cross-bar is broken).

The second sword is much more ornate. It has an engraved gold hilt with carved ivory grips. The scabbard is covered in black fish-skin with gold mountings. The 32-inch blade is marked 'VR'.

Both swords have a very gentle curve.

Fig 22: Forage cap and belt

Officer's forage cap, pouch and shoulder belt, circa 1890. All are of scarlet cloth with gold lace and ornaments. The crown on the pouch also has some silver embroidery.

Fig 23: Patrol Jacket

Worn by officers in undress from 1876 to 1904. The jacket was dark blue cloth, edged in black Astrakhan, and laced and braided with black mohair of the regimental pattern ('Austrian Wave'). In 1895 the turn-down collar was altered to a 'stand-up' type.

Fig 24:

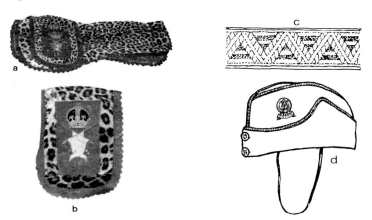

a *The last type of full dress saddle cover (Queen's crown).*
b *King's crown variation of the same pattern of leopard skin.*
c *The 'Austrian Wave'. The lace pattern of the 15th Hussars.*
d *Officer's field service cap (scarlet, braided gold).*

Fig 26: Other Ranks Horse Equipment, circa 1895

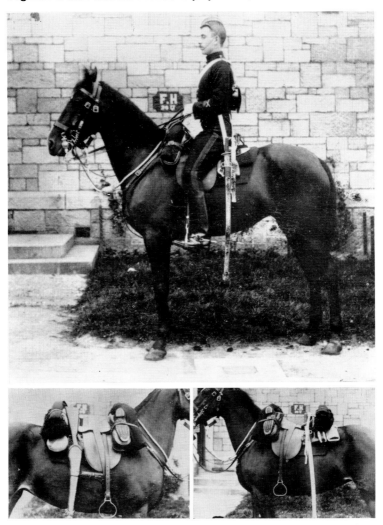

The mounted figure shows the saddle for Drill Order.

The two detail photographs present something of an enigma. As the equipment does not include corn bag, canvas bucket, picketing peg or blanket it is unlikely to be full Marching Order. It is possibly equipment assembled for outpost or picket duty.

Fig 27: Undress Tunics, circa 1900

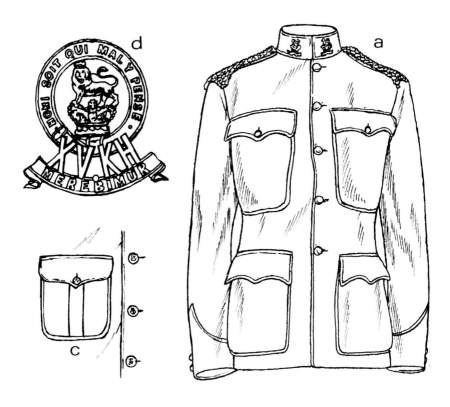

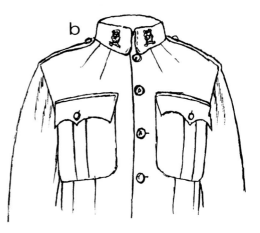

a *Officer's blue serge frock.*

b *Officer's khaki frock had fall-down collar and different pocket flaps to that of other ranks (shown in Colour Plate 8). It was also a deeper shade of khaki.*

c *The smaller breast pocket of other ranks blue serge in relation to position of the three middle buttons. Unlike the officer's model it had pocket pleats, no hip pockets, a shallower collar and no cuff buttons.*

d *The field service cap badge. The collar badge was the lion standing on the crown over a scroll inscribed 'Merebimur'.*

Fig 28: Stable Dress, circa 1900
(from contemporary photographs)

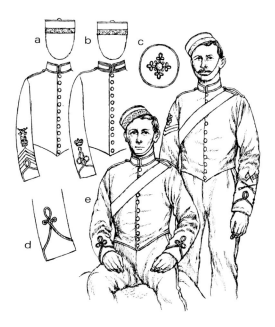

a *Sergeant Trumpeter (title changed from Trumpet Major in 1881). The scarlet cap has gold braid around the top and the normal NCO width of gold lace rather than the wider lace of bandsmen. No braid is shown around the edge of the jacket. All decoration is in gold.*

b *Regimental Sergeant-Major—as in the previous figure but with a double row of collar braid and a distinctive Austrian cuff knot.*

c *Braid design on top of other ranks cap.*

d *Detail of bandsman's cuff knot.*

e *Seated figure is a bandsman. Note wider cap lace of different pattern and braid around edge of jacket. The standing Corporal wears marksman and signaller badges on the left arm only. All lace and braid on both figures is yellow.*

Youthful drummer of the 15th Hussars, circa 1890

These are the 'marching out' drum banners, less ornate than the full dress ones shown on page 8. The banners have a red ground with blue garter and scroll. Lettering and decoration are in gold. The crown in the centre of the garter is silver.

Drum Banner of 1820-1830

Scarlet ground, gold scrolls, crown and fringe. Silver cypher and flags (with gold fleur-de-lis).

Appendices

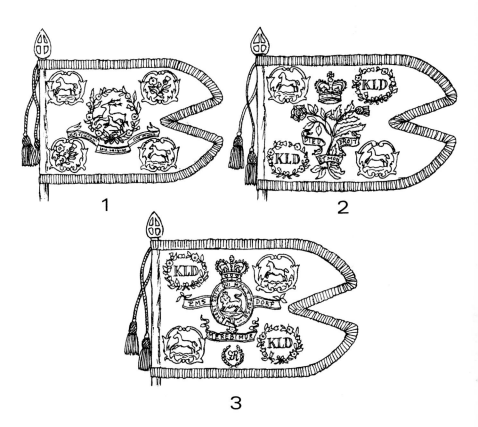

1

2

3

Guidons

Technically, the 15th should have ceased to carry standards when they were converted from Light Dragoons to Hussars around 1806. Inspection Returns of the two years following, however, give the Regiment as being in possession of standards, although they may not have been used.

In 1805 the 15th Light Dragoons were listed in Inspection Returns as having five standards. Four standards were presented in 1800 and it was 1834 before a General Order officially abolishing standards for hussars was issued.

Drawings made of the Guidons of the 15th about 1807 show them as having rounded ends like those of heavy cavalry, rather than the regulation swallow tails of light cavalry.

The three Guidons illustrated are based on the 1807 notes and are coloured as follows:

1 *Regimental Guidon, 1760:* Green ground, white horses on red patches and rose and thistle in natural colours on red patches, set around the centre device. This consists of a white hound attacking a brown stag all on a red

patch, surrounded by a natural coloured wreath of roses and thistles. The scroll underneath is white and bears a black legend. The fringe is silver.

2 *King's Guidon, 1760:* Crimson ground with natural colour rose and thistle intertwined. Silver crown and scroll (lettered black). Green quarter patches 'KLD' in silver (natural colour wreath). White horses with silver border surround. The Guidon is fringed silver.

3 *King's Guidon, circa 1800:* Crimson silk ground, fringed gold. Scarlet centre patch with gold lion surrounded by blue garter and scrolls all lettered gold. The Royal Cypher below the centre scroll is a gold 'GR' on a scarlet ground surrounded by green laurels. The four surrounding patches are scarlet with the 'KLD' in gold (natural colour wreath) and the horse is white with a gold surround.

According to regulations these quarter patches are in reverse order but the contemporary sketch shows them as described. There were three regimental standards. These were blue silk with basically the same decorations, except that in the scarlet patch below the centre scroll in place of the Royal Cypher were the gold numerals 1, 2 and 3 respectively.

Swords of the 15th Hussars

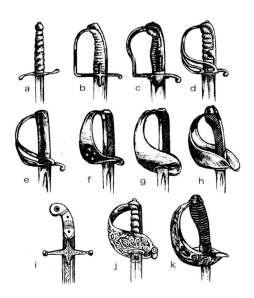

a	*1760*	**b**	*1775*	**c**	*1795*	**d**	*1829*
e	*1853*	**f**	*1864*	**g**	*1899*	**h**	*1908*

i *Officer's Mameluke, 1820*   **j** *Officers 1896*   **k** *Officers 1912*

The dates given are when the swords were generally in use. Portraits often show earlier models of swords being worn with later uniforms. It was also often impossible to supply troops in the field with new model weapons and consequently they were issued much later than officially stated.

Officers used similar models to a, b, c and d, but often smaller and with finer workmanship.

Carbines of the 15th Hussars

In order from top to bottom the weapons shown are the following:

First Model: Flintlock, a straight bar and sliding ring fixed to the inner side to attach to the shoulder belt. Barrel length 29 inches. After 1800. flintlock, a curved bar for the sliding ring. Barrel length 21 inches.

1825: Flintlock, fixed ring to replace the sliding ring, back sight fitted. Barrel length 15 inches.

1830: Percussion cap. Barrel length 15 inches.

1862: Snider breech loader, two steel loops on the stock replacing the sliding bar and ring. A leather shoulder sling for use when dismounted. Barrel length 24 inches.

1878. Martini Henry carbine.

1892: Lee Metford.

1901: Lee Enfield.

Pistols were carried by all ranks until May 1839, when they were discontinued except for officers, Sergeant-Majors and Trumpeters who retained one each.